746.9209044

This book is to be returned on or before

i

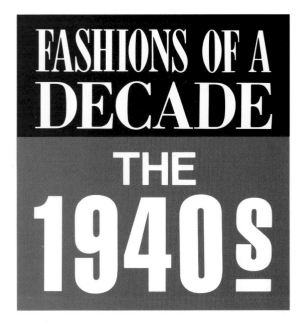

FASHIONS OF A
DECADE
THE
1940s

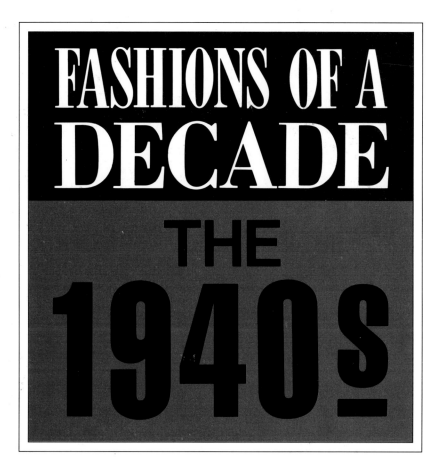

FASHIONS OF A DECADE

THE 1940s

Patricia Baker

Series Editors: Valerie Cumming and
Elane Feldman
Original Illustrations by Robert Price

B.T. Batsford · London

Contents

Text design by David Stanley
Jacket design by David Stanley
Composition by Latimer Trend
Manufactured by Bookbuilders Ltd
Printed in Hong Kong

Published by B.T. Batsford Ltd
4 Fitzhardinge Street
London W1H 0AH

A CIP catalogue record for this book is available from the British Library.

ISBN 0 7134 6639 1

THE 40s

Fashion wasn't grabbing the headlines in the newspapers of 1940. The silhouette for both menswear and women's clothing was largely unchanged from the previous couple of years. As the forties began the female shape consisted of wide, padded shoulders; a narrow natural waistline; thin hips; and a skirt that fell just below the knee. For men also the line fell in an inverted triangle from square shoulders down to the waist and hips, with heavy shoes providing a counterbalance for both men and women.

Accessories were still essential. Hats were popular and styles varied, including those tipped over women's foreheads or planted firmly on the back of the head. During the war, however, hats were increasingly replaced by fabric head scarves and turbans, especially for women involved in war work in factories. Hats themselves were one of the casualties of war. For a time there was also a vogue for ''snoods'' made of fabric or of knitted or crocheted yarn. These were worn to hold fashionable long hair in place at the nape of the neck.

Handbags took the form of small box bags, especially in black plastic patent with a mirror in the lid. For daytime, over-the-shoulder bags were carried and large "clutch" bags without handles were widely seen. "Crushed" suede gloves with flaring cuffs were popular for daywear. These were elbow-length but worn casually pushed down the arm, hence the name "crushed". For evening wear shirred rayon jersey gloves were considered a glamour accessory around 1944, as fabric replaced leather.

Despite this continuity, there had already been the occasional hint of change on the catwalks of the fashion salons. Both in Paris and New York, a number of designers had been experimenting with a new silhouette, based on the waist. However, there were more serious things to think about.

Women in uniform (1): Canada Dry Ginger Ale salutes American servicewomen in 1944.

Women in uniform (2): Keep 'em rolling. This woman in uniform does her bit on the Pennysylvania Railroad. The passengers wear a noteworthy selection of wartime styles. Note in particular the variety of different headgear worn by both sexes.

The World at War

The months of uncertainty and apprehension leading up to the war were at last over; the real thing had begun. Europe was in bloody turmoil. Adolf Hitler's army had invaded Poland on September 1, 1939. Two days later, the British and French governments declared war on the German Third Reich. By the time the United States entered the conflict after the Japanese attack on Pearl Harbor, Hawaii, on December 7, 1941, Norway, Denmark, Holland, Belgium, France, Yugoslavia and Greece had fallen into Hitler's hands, and the European regions of the Soviet Union had narrowly escaped the same fate.

It looked as if Britain's days were also numbered. Although the planes of the German Luftwaffe (air force) had been beaten off in the Battle of Britain (September 15, 1940), bombs continued to fall on the major British industrial cities and sea ports, so that eight months later one in every six households in London no longer had a home, or even worse, one in four in Plymouth. To hamper enemy bombers, streetlights were switched off and everyone was asked to conceal houselights, by putting up black material at windows. After the Japanese attacked Pearl Harbor, Americans too had to observe "black out" rules. Bombs weren't the only problem: it was widely believed that chemical or gas warfare would be used against civilian populations, so gas masks were issued and carried by everyone. The fashionable London store Harvey Nichols advertized specially designed hooded gas protection suits for women stating: "made of pure oiled silk . . . in dawn, apricot, rose, amethyst, eau-de-nil green and pastel pink. The wearer can cover a distance of two hundred yards through mustard gas and the suit can be slipped over ordinary clothes in thirty-five seconds . . ."

Utility wartime fashions for the British store Berkatex by Norman Hartnell, 1943.

Rationing

All military personnel had to be equipped with weapons and clothing, and this meant factories on both sides of the Atlantic had to swing from producing consumer goods to war goods. In early 1941 the effects of this programme were felt in Britain, and later in North America. It seemed that everything was rationed or was going to be.

The doublet jacket

brown and white sharkskin suit
for Spring excitement

Duran

I. Magnin & Co.
California

In 1943 even bathwater was limited in Britain; only 5″ were allowed in the tub regardless of how many people shared the same water. No wonder advertisements for deodorants suddenly increased.

In Britain, clothes rationing started in earnest in June 1941. At first 66 coupons a year were given to each adult, but this was quickly reduced to 48, and then to 36 in 1945. Eighteen coupons had to be handed over when purchasing a woman's tweed suit; 11 for a woollen dress; for a skirt 7; and another 5 for a blouse or cardigan; it's not surprising separates were seen as the best value. A new pair of shoes meant sacrificing 7 precious coupons, 2 coupons less if one bought wooden soled shoes, but care had to be taken when drying them out after heavy rain, or they split.

Extra coupons were available on the black market, the illegal trade in goods in short supply, and it was possible to buy some non-regulated fabric and garments. Supplies became increasingly limited, and the price high, not only because of the scarcity, but also because a purchase tax was applied to such non-coupon items. If you were caught trying to avoid the regulations, the fines were heavy. Lady Astor found that out in 1943 after she had persuaded her American friends to send over clothes for her; she was fined £50, ten times the amount of a lady's suit bought with coupons. Even three years after the war in Europe had ended, a London seamstress was

Stand Up To It! Practical wear for the Blitz, from London's Harvey Nicolls store. Note the prominence given to the shelter suit – an all-in-one garment for air-raid shelter wear.

Sweaters – A Health Hazard?

One of the most popular garments of the 1940s was the sweater. But at the Vought-Sikorsky Aircraft Corporation in America, 53 women were sent home for wearing them. At first the management explained that the ban was on moral grounds – for being too sexy. But when the union pointed out that sweaters were considered suitable for office workers, the company cited safety reasons. The National Safety Council confirmed that sweaters might easily catch fire because they attracted static electricity, and if caught in machinery they would not rip and so might pull the wearer in too. Hollywood's Ann Sheridan, known as the "Oomph girl", joined the dispute and said that sweaters themselves weren't bad, but a little girl in a big sweater might be a safety hazard, while a big girl in a small sweater might be a moral one. Finally the Conciliation Service of the US Labor Department had to intervene.

Post-war, pre New Look. The military influence is strong in this 1945 suit by Magnin of Los Angeles.

COATS — SUITS — FROCKS

Nicoll Clothes

A.28
K.351   L.211   F.180

'Nicoll Clothes'
41-45 Warwick Street, W.I
Telephone: Regent 1951

Outerwear from Nina Ricci, 1943. The elaborate headgear so common during the war is teamed here with a waistline that prefigures the New Look.

Wartime Utility fashions from Britain's Norman Hartnell, June 1943. Using top designer names became a way of making standardized designs more attractive. Strangely, it also meant that some women became better dressed as a result of wartime restrictions.

Chanel's War

Although the designer Gabrielle "Coco" Chanel closed her fashion house a year before the war started and disappeared from the fashion scene, her activities still caused controversy. In part this was due to her love affair with a high Nazi official – but she was also a vocal supporter of the Vichy regime, despised by many French people and not recognized by the Allies. She regarded members of the French Resistance as criminals, since they were breaking the terms of the armistice that France had asked for and arranged with the Germans. These actions and attitudes meant that after the war Chanel had difficulty in reopening her salon for many years. It finally reopened in 1954.

Day dress from the House of Lelong, 1943. Again, the hat provides a point of departure from the otherwise quite severely practical tailoring.

taken to court for embroidering floral motifs on lingerie, seen as an unpatriotic waste. Not even the royal family was exempt from rationing. For her wedding to Philip Mountbatten (Duke of Edinburgh) in 1947, Princess Elizabeth was merely given an extra allowance, totalling 100 coupons. The government also specified that no "enemy" products were to be used for the wedding dress, which meant the British designer Norman Hartnell could not use Japanese seed-pearls nor Italian silk.

In the United States, restrictions and embargos were also having an effect: nylon hose was replacing silk because of the shortage caused by the ban on Japanese silk thread; nylon itself was also required for military uses. The US Production Board issued Limitations Orders, such as L-85 in 1942. This aimed to save 15% of domestic fabric production and 40–50 million pounds of wool as well as to freeze fashion, "thus forestalling any radical change . . . making existing clothes obsolete." As with the British regulations, the L-85 order specified the amount of fabric, jacket (men's and women's) and skirt-lengths, trouser leg and skirt-widths, the number of buttons, pleats and trimmings to be used. Cuffs, double yokes, patch pockets and attached coat-hoods were all banned, part of a general "no fabric on fabric" rule. The height of high heels was fixed at a maximum of $1\frac{1}{2}''$ in the United States, whereas the British Government was less restrictive, allowing $2''$. The manufacture of metal zippers was severely hit as the metal was needed for armament production. Sequins, however, were classed as unessential to the American war effort, and their supply and use were unrestricted. All the American clothing restrictions were lifted on VE (Victory in Europe) Day, May 8, 1945, with the US price control chief, Chester Bowles, announcing on the radio: "Now you can take your gasoline and fuel oil coupons and paste them in your memory book. Rationing has been lifted, too, on canned fruit and vege-

Sweethearts of the Forces! Contestants gather in New York for the title of 'Service Cover Girl of 1944.'

tables." With that, the orders for 187 million books of green and white ration coupons were cancelled, but the price freeze that had been introduced in 1943 went on for another year. In Britain rationing continued for three more painful years, until 1949, with some restrictions only removed in 1955.

Wartime swing: Benny Goodman and his orchestra perform in white tuxedo jackets, black ties and trousers and red carnations.

A War Diet

The New Year 1940 was marked in Britain by the introduction of food rationing. Each adult was allowed 12 ounces of sugar, 4 ounces butter and 4 ounces of bacon or ham every week. By the end of that summer, one pound of meat per person was permitted, but the butter ration had been halved. The restrictions were quickly extended to include tea and cheese. Eggs too were strictly rationed: one advertisement in a local paper ran "Wanted: Egg timer, sentimental reasons. Wanted: Egg, same reason." The end of the war meant no immediate relief. In fact bread rationing was brought in and the basic food allowance were further cut so that by 1948, the average person was worse off than during the war.

Rationing for the Parisians under Nazi occupation began in September 1940. Each adult was allowed 12 ounces of bread a day, but only about 5 ounces of meat and cheese for a whole month. Sugar and coffee were like gold-dust. Within six months rice, noodles, fats (including soaps), fish, tobacco, textiles and wine were all rationed. By December 1944, fuel was so short that cooking was permitted for only one to two hours at lunchtime and an hour in the evening. It was another four-and-a-half years before rationing was lifted.

Easy does it...Have a Coke

...relax with *the pause that refreshes*

There's no gloom to broom work when the whole family tackles spring cleaning. Especially when right at hand in the family icebox there's delicious, frosty Coca-Cola. *Have a Coke* just naturally means "Let's take time off and enjoy *the pause that refreshes.*" Whether you're cleaning house or holding open house for friends, Coca-Cola goes with the friendly spirit of good-humored, hospitable family ways.

Coke = Coca-Cola

"Coca-Cola" and its abbreviation "Coke" are the registered trade-marks which distinguish the product of The Coca-Cola Company.

Serve **Coca-Cola** at home

"Got Any Gum, Chum?"

With the United States entering the war in 1942, increasing numbers of American servicemen were stationed in Britain before being moved to the battlefront. It quickly became apparent that the two cultures, although sharing the same language, were very different and both governments offered advice on codes of behaviour. The American GI was advised: "Don't comment on politics. Don't try to tell the British that America won the last war. NEVER criticize the King or Queen. Don't criticize food, beer or cigarettes . . . Use your head before you sound off, and remember how long the British alone have held Hitler off. If the British look dowdy and badly dressed it is not because they do not like good clothes or know how to wear them. All clothes are rationed. Old clothes are good form."

The British newspapers asked their readers to remember that the Americans ". . . are foreigners . . . and that the mistakes they make are likely to spring from too quick enthusiasm and too little background; that though we may be spiritually far more civilized, materially they have the advantage."

Topsiders (as worn by the young men in the foreground), shorts, sleeveless sweaters. The American casual look is linked here with the growing thirst for Coca Cola worldwide.

Young American styles: Bobby sox, plaid skirts, and linen jackets with the characteristic wide shoulders of the period.

From America to the world. A buttoned-up look for tomorrow's traveller in 1945.

War-time Production

The British Board of Trade issued the following information to shopowners, presumably to advise them how to deal with complaints from customers about scarcity of goods:

    CORSETS become parachutes and chinstraps
    LACE CURTAINS become sand-fly netting
    CARPETS become webbing equipment
    TOILET PREPARATIONS become anti-gas ointments
    SAUCEPANS become steel helmets
    COMBS become eyeshields

Hollywood, fashion and the war (1): *Lifeboat*. Socialite Tallulah Bankhead plays a fashion journalist adrift in a lifeboat with eight other survivors from a torpedo attack. Her impeccable two-piecce suit seems to have easily survived its immersion in the sea.

Hollywood, fashion and the war (2): *Casablanca*. Uniforms, a square-shouldered suit for Ingrid Bergman, and Humphrey Bogart's snap-brim hat with his overcoat belt knotted, not fastened.

Fashion in Wartime

With the German occupation of Paris in the summer of 1940, the fashion houses in Paris under the leadership of Lucien Lelong fought for survival and to protect their employees from being sent to enemy factories. They were no longer the second largest exporting industry in France. For all intents and purposes, Paris was totally cut off, and suddenly American and British designers were the trend-setters with an important part to play in keeping public morale high. No longer designing solely for a small, exclusive clientele, their work was to encourage a positive response to the strict regulations on clothing. In Britain, fashion designers, including those who had left France before the fall of Paris, came together in the Incorporated Society of London Fashion Designers (ISLFD), working with the government's Board of Trade. Similarly, designers in the United States involved themselves in the war effort, either directly as in the case of Mainbocher, who designed the WAVES (Women Accepted for Voluntary Emergency Service) uniform, or working within the government stipulations as laid out in the L-85 order. American fashion journalists facing life without Paris, suddenly realized the talent lying on their own door-steps. The American fashion houses began to receive the recognition they richly deserved. It was a short-lived but sweet triumph. Of course for the average person, Hollywood films offered the usual inspiration, although studio costume designers had to work under the same fabric restrictions. A number of appeals were made by the government to the designers and stars to help the war effort by promoting various styles.

Women became increasingly adept at making do, taking garments apart and restyling them. The media constantly offered advice and hints such as making coats out of old blankets. Women were also encouraged to aid the war effort in other ways. They were told: "use it up, wear it out, make it do or do without." In New York City there was a drive for old furs that were then made into fur lined waistcoats for the merchant marine. There were long lines of customers for everything. And with so many men on both sides of the Atlantic drafted into military service, only women could ease the very real shortage of labour, both on the farm and in the factories. Quickly, the traditional barriers clearly defining "men's work" and "women's work" and social conventions relating to dressing up for certain activities collapsed. Dungarees (blue denim pants), trousers and one-piece coveralls as women's wear were socially acceptable at work, and safety regulations linked with scarce supplies dictated the new hairstyles. Although differences in wages remained for some time, many women enjoyed the greater opportunities that war work offered. They were now expected and encouraged to play a full and active role in society and this was reflected in romantic fiction and films of the time, such as *His Girl Friday* (1940), in which the square-shouldered, short-skirted heroine was frequently portrayed working towards self-fulfilment and, during that quest, finding the man of her dreams; there was never a hint that to keep him, she was expected to give up her search.

Wartime non-utility clothes in Britain followed the styles of the official utility designers.

"MARGO"
Exquisitely tailored Frock, intricate detail on bodice, pleats front of skirt. In pastel shades of blue, green, rose and beige. Sizes 38, 40, 42 and 44 in.   **£9.11.2**
(11 coupons)

Model Gowns
FIRST FLOOR

"YVONNE"
Attractive Frock, cowl neck, jumper effect, unusual V design on bodice and pocket. In pastel shades of blue, green, rose and beige. Sizes 38, 40, 42 and 44 in.
(11 coupons)   **£9.2.5**

"JEANNE"
Extremely neat Jumper Suit, shirt collar and buttoned-through front, insets on bodice. In pastel shades of blue, green, rose and beige. Sizes 38, 40, 42 and 44 in.
(14 coupons)   **£10.18.11**

WHEN HOSPITALITY'S IN THE AIR...

IT'S MAXWELL HOUSE COFFEE TIME!

There's good cheer and a warm welcome in every cup of this richer, finer coffee!

● Whether it's open house for scores of service men ... or a quiet evening at home with a friend or two ... hospitality time is Maxwell House Coffee Time! This famous coffee, bought and enjoyed by more people than any other brand in the world, adds a gracious note of welcome and friendly good cheer to any occasion.

Fine Latin-American coffees are skillfully blended to bring you—in Maxwell House—a coffee you'll *completely* enjoy, and be proud to serve your guests. Manizales coffees for mellowness ... Bucaramangas for full body ... Medellins for rich flavor ... Central and South American coffees for vigor. Then Radiant Roasting develops the *full* flavor of every coffee bean in this famous blend. In victory bag or vacuum jar, Maxwell House Coffee is truly "Good to the Last Drop!"

Good to the last drop!

A Product of General Foods

IT'S MAXWELL HOUSE COFFEE TIME ON THE AIR, TOO ... THE HILARIOUS FRANK MORGAN SHOW ... NBC, THURSDAY NIGHT

Winning the Peace

The end of the war brought its own problems. The process of demobilization, releasing millions of men from military service, began, and finding work for them was an urgent priority. Suddenly, the women workers were no longer needed. The British government began a crash programme persuading them that their place, happiness and future were in the home. The men themselves had to readjust to home-life and the realization that in their absence, the womenfolk had managed quite well without them. Again popular romantic fiction caught the spirit of the times; in the British

The fashionable image of servicemen is harnessed here to promote the sale of coffee, February 1945. Note also how the waitress has her hair tied back in a style similar to that suggested for factory work.

The end in sight: US and Soviet troops link up at Torgau on the river Elbe in Germany. Military clothing was to prove a major influence on post-war menswear.

Only Angels Have Wings

For many, the war-time pilot seemed to be the hero of the hour, especially after the Battle of Britain. As Gary Cooper showed in the film *For Whom the Bell Tolls* (1943), he was the 20th-century version of the medieval knight, with his gauntlets, helmet and protective clothing, going forth alone or with a few friends to vanquish the enemy and put the world to rights. His heavy sheepskin jacket, called the Shearling among American airmen and the Irvin in Royal Air Force circles, set him aside from the men of the other services. Everyone wanted to be identified with him. Even Charles James, the Anglo-American designer, suggested his pre-war heavily quilted ladies' jacket, made of Chinese silk, was the inspiration behind the later WWII Shearling USAF jacket.

All the news that's fit to print. The ultra-brief bikini swimsuit makes its entrance, summer 1946 – complete with newsprint motifs.

Baring the Midriff

The US government should be thanked for the introduction of the two-piece bathing suit. In 1943, it ordered that the fabric used in women's swimwear was to be reduced by one-tenth, as part of its policy to save textile wastage. The little "skirt" panel of the one-piece was the first victim of the cuts and then the one-piece itself was attacked. The two-piece and the midriff were born. Three years later, the American nuclear tests carried out on Bikini Atoll in the South Pacific caused the little-known Parisian designer, Louis Reard, to name his latest swimwear design the bikini. He said later that this was because the name symbolized "The Ultimate." In a similar way, the incredible power of the atomic bomb, as shown at Hiroshima in 1945, led to a rash of "atomic" products such as Atomic Dry-cleaners, Atomic Hair-restorer and even an Atomic pudding.

magazine *My Weekly* (May 18, 1946) the hero realized that: "He was no good. He wasn't needed. A woman, his own wife, stood in his shoes and they seemed to fit her very well."

Each man, on leaving military service in Britain, was given a basic wardrobe, including a suit, shirt, tie, socks, hat and a pair of shoes, and sent on his way. Menswear didn't undergo any radical change from the pre-war to post-war eras. It has been suggested that this was because the tailors and manufacturers, after half a decade of war, weren't able to make anything else but a suit based on late thirties styling. Or it's possible that men themselves, feeling a little insecure in their new civilian lives, preferred this conservative look, which had almost a military conformity about it. There were a couple of exceptions. The zoot-suiters and spivs revelled in their exaggerated style of dress, but the general public disapproved of such displays and, in Britain in particular, it was associated with the seamy side of life and racketeering.

In the United States, rationing and restrictions were quickly lifted and the country moved speedily from full-scale armaments manufacture into mass domestic production, enjoying the increased prosperity that war work had brought for many. In Europe and Great Britain, the process took much longer. The war had destroyed not only factories and houses but also ports and rail yards. The national economies were in grave trouble and Britain itself was virtually bankrupt. Rationing continued and indeed was more rigorously applied.

For the first few years after the war, there was uncertainty about the direction fashion was to take. Some American designers responded with designs of great luxury and femininity, such as these 1946 evening dresses from (left to right) Hattie Carnegie, Adele Simpson, Nettie Rosenstein and Muriel King. The appearance of full skirts and narrow waists presages the coming of the New Look in 1947.

The Bobby Sox Idol

The formal orchestration of the Big Band was losing public appeal in favour of a new "intimacy" with the radio listeners, as Bing Crosby was showing what complete mastery of the microphone could achieve. As Bing crooned his way into the dreams of adult women on both sides of the Atlantic, Frank Sinatra became the idol of teenage girls, the "Sultan of Swoon", as his press agent put it. He had started work singing for the big bands where he learned, as he said, to "play" his voice just like musicians played their instruments, and his artistry in phrasing a song has never deserted him. He explained his immense success in the early 1940s by saying "It was the war years, and there was great loneliness. And I was the boy in every corner drugstore who'd gone off, drafted to the war. That was all."

Don't call them teenagers – yet. Bobby sox, pleated skirts, sweaters, round collars, tied back hair. Plus penny loafers, as worn by the girl on the right.

King of the crooners. Frank Sinatra in wide lapels, top-pleat trousers and big cuff-links.

Rainwear. Austin Reed of London's version of the man's overcoat, trilby hat, umbrella and kid gloves. Broad-shouldered styles such as these were widely popular in the post-war forties.

Capes and gloves: New Look outerwear of 1948.

A Barbaric New Era?

It was only in the last years of the war that the scale of horror began to be realized. With the Allied advance into Europe, the true nature of Nazi concentration camps was uncovered. The news and the horrifying pictures stunned everyone. It seemed impossible that humans could carry out such cruelty on their fellows. Almost six million people died in what is now called the Holocaust. Returning prisoners of war from Japanese camps showed that inhumanity was not confined to Europe and, as the atrocities suffered by hundreds of thousands of Chinese showed, not just against Europeans. The atomic bombs dropped by the Allies on Hiroshima and then Nagasaki in early August 1945 unleashed a monstrous new power of destruction.

Dramatic stripes and decorative gathers lend excitement to the latest stretch swimsuits from Jantzen, 1948.

Back to prosperity: the 1949 Studebaker.

Enter Monsieur Dior

With the liberation of Paris, the work of the French fashion designers under German occupation came to light, and it wasn't greeted with wild enthusiasm and approval. It seemed that while everyone else had been frugally saving and heeding official regulations – even Hollywood had largely obeyed them – the French designers had continued as if there weren't a war. And when Christian Dior unveiled his "Corolla", or flower-like, collection in 1947 – quickly named the New Look – the post-war murmurs about past collaboration with the Germans erupted into roars of disapproval. Government officials in London and Washington, taking one look at the amount of fabric used in the Dior dresses, warned that the newly reborn post-war economies could be fatally damaged if such extravagance was copied.

However, Dior had timed it perfectly. Women on both sides of the Atlantic were eager for a change. They had had enough of the square shoulders, short skirts, dark colours; it all looked so military, so functional, and so dull. They fell for Dior's curvaceous line, accentuating the bust, the waist, the hips and the ankles, and the sheer extravagance of yards and yards of fabric.

New Look in New York. Christian Dior arrives by sea to promote his designs in the USA, April 1948.

Perhaps the wartime fashion designers had done their job too well. From serving a small elite clientele, they now enjoyed enormous public prestige and influence over a much wider section of society. Where in the thirties, fashion had little immediate and direct impact on the general public, now cheap mass garment production, a result of reorganizing to meet war demand, meant everyone could have copies of model designs quickly and at a fraction of the original cost. Although the established clientele was still important for a fashion house, increasingly it was the fashion journalist who decided its fate, by giving the thumbs up or down on the collections. As a way of reaping as much benefit as possible from publicity and to offset occasional hostile

Suffering for beauty. Models lace each other into the tight corsets demanded by the New Look silhouette.

New Look influence. A gun-metal and pale blue knitted tweed coat of 1949 by Hardy Amies. Note also the high-heeled court shoes.

criticism of a certain collection, everything from scarves to underwear and perfume were sold under the designer's name to get cash flowing into the fashion house. By the end of the decade the fashion houses had began in earnest in play the "name game" and promote the cult of the individual designer.

New materials – rainwear in "Koroseal" from B.F. Goodrich. The war provided a spur to materials technology.

A 1947 evening dress in white chiffon with a leopard-print bodice by America's Norman Norell. The New Look shape can be seen in the nipped waist and accentuated hips.

"New Looks" for cars: the 1949 Oldsmobile points the way forward to the streamlined American auto styling of the 1950s.

26

V for Victory

War Work

As the factories moved into munition and other war production, consumer goods became scarce and rationing was the only fair way of distributing limited supplies to everyone. Certain raw materials were not available and sacrifices had to be made. General shortages led to some ingenious solutions.

Clothes rationing started in the United Kingdom in June 1941 with both garments and fabrics manufactured under Utility regulations, issued by the government Board of Trade. These specified the amount, quality and type of fabric, jacket length, width of skirt or trouser leg, of hems, the number of buttons, pleats and trimmings in every garment. Small pattern motifs or certain monochrome colours (like Flag Red and Victory Blue) were specified as this also reduced wastage in making up.

The US L-85 order was geared to save 15 percent of domestic fabric production by banning such items as cuffs, full skirts, patch pockets, knife pleats and attached coathoods. Order M-217 conserved leather and limited shoes to six colours while laces and some kinds of embroidery were restricted by order L-116. Ten percent of fabric had to be saved from women's bathing suits, leading to the two-piece suit. As the *Wall Street Journal* reported ". . . the saving has been effected – in the region of the midriff. The two piece bathing suit now is tied in with the war as closely as the zipperless dress and the pleatless skirt."

Given the widespread difficulties in obtaining entire new wardrobes, accessories such as hats, gloves and

handbags became very important for many women. Dickeys, that is collars, some with extended shirt fronts, were often worn beneath sweaters instead of a blouse; as were jabots, often in the form of a standing band collar with attached ruffle at the front.

From 1943 the British public was bombarded by campaigns asking them to make do and mend. Women were exhorted to knit – or sew – for victory. Wool was rationed so this meant unra-

Veronica Lake and Alan Ladd in *This Gun for Hire.* **Lake was asked to tie up her long, flowing tresses, as they provided a bad example to women war workers required to keep their hair neatly tied up.**

velling existing knit-wear, and redyeing the yarn. Leaflets explained how blankets could be made into coats and how men's trousers could become a skirt or a child's garment.

Designed for War

In the US dress manufacturers had to design their styles to be worn without girdles as the use of rubber in girdles was banned. One dress manufacturer advertised: "No girdle required for this dress . . . with no fastenings (zippers gone to war) adjustable at waist and bust." Another ad read: "Duration suit: both jacket and skirt . . . are adjustable at the waistline; designed for war with or without a girdle."

While some corset manufacturers designed rubberless girdles (one even went back to using whalebone) women were being advised to adjust to life without their restraining help. *McCall's* Washington newsletter warned: "Just what the lack of girdles will eventually do to styles is anyone's guess, but Washington's experts don't hold out much hope for a return to solid, hefty bulges."

With increasing numbers of women drawn into war work the effects of the demands of safety were noticeable. Several famous companies had designers suggest safe, attractive outfits; for instance Vera Maxwell created the coveralls for women working for Sperry Gyroscope. *McCall's Magazine* in 1942 listed some of the possible advantages: "The girl in the defense factory really has all the luck. She wears a coverall for work and thereby saves clothes, time, money and nervous energy. And look at all the nice green cash she picks out of the envelope each week!"

Women were urged to have their hair cut short in the new Vingle (a close-cropped haircut), the Victory Roll or the Liberty Cut, which needed to be cut only once every three months. This served more than one purpose: hairpins were unavailable, hats needed coupons and women in war-time factories were being badly injured as a result of getting their hair caught in machinery. The immensely popular "peekaboo" hairstyle of American film-star Veronica Lake, with a cascade of hair over one eye, was thought

The military braid hairstyle, approved for women in wartime.

hazardous. When appealed to, she patriotically, and very publicly, changed to an upswept style, in the hope of persuading her fans to copy her.

Seams an Illusion . . .

Silk and nylon stockings vanished from British shops in December 1940 and the problem was also felt in America. Trousers hid the absence of hose, but one could resort to Cyclax Stocking-less Cream, or other forms of leg makeup, the illusion of hose being completed by drawing "seams" down the back of the legs with an eyebrow pencil.

Soap, for both personal washing and laundry was like gold dust in Britain,

where the ration was 4 ounces a month. In the US the War Production Board conducted a survey among American women asking what cosmetics were absolutely vital to their morale, and it was decided that bath oil was essential while bath salts were not. The women agreed that face powder, lipstick, rouge and deodorants were very crucial.

The British actress Ruby Miller made sense when she suggested that women wore light-coloured clothing when travelling home in the blackout, to prevent traffic accidents, but it didn't appeal to the average British woman. Instead, there was a fad for luminous lapel brooches and pins, in the shape of flowers.

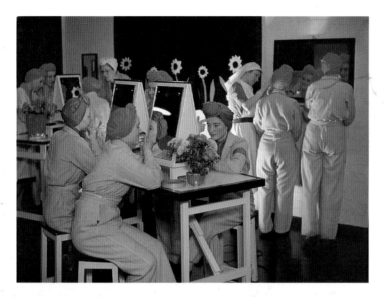

Ordnance factory workers in
overalls, with hair tied up in scarves.

USAF Mustang pilots being briefed
before a mission. After the war,
pilot's uniforms were to prove a key
influence on male dress.

Slacks, blouse and jacket, and
flat-heeled shoes: a practical look for
working women.

Sea, sun and sand – and the
two-piece bathing suit. The fabric
covering the midriff was a war-time
casualty.

Paris Under Fire

Occupation

In June 1940 the Germans marched into Paris and occupied the city; they did not leave until August 1944. The French government fled and was taken over by Marshal Pétain, a veteran of the First World War. He asked the Germans for an armistice, and it was agreed that a French government, under Pétain, could rule over the unoccupied part of the country. This was known as the Vichy government, but many French people did not recognize its authority as it cooperated with the Germans. Paris and the northern and western parts of France were placed under German rule. Here, as everywhere under Nazi rule, Jewish people were rounded up and deported to concentration and forced labour camps.

Paris fashion houses were to survive the Nazi occupation of Paris thanks to one man, Lucien Lelong, the head of Chambre Syndicale de la Couture Parisienne (the Paris Fashion Syndicate). A number of chief designers and Jewish manufacturers had left at the outbreak of hostilities and in 1940 Berlin High Command ordered the closure of the CSCP and the transfer of the fashion houses and designers to Berlin and Vienna; the Third Reich wanted to have fashion centres it believed worthy of its leader. Lelong argued that the French fashion industry relied not only on the star designers but on everyone else as well, including manufacturers and suppliers; that expertise would be lost. The order was withdrawn, the Chambre reopened, and Pierre Balmain and Christian Dior moved to join Lelong. In all, 20 fashion houses kept their doors open, and 112,000 skilled workers were excused compulsory work in enemy factories.

German officers and their wives pay a wartime visit to a French racecourse. Life went on, despite the occupation.

Wedges and Berets

Lelong also pointed out that American clients would bring in much needed dollars (though in fact most stayed away for the duration of the war). With the introduction of rationing in France in 1941, the fashion houses were given special fabric allowances, and permission to sell their garments outside coupon restrictions. Prices soared not only because of the increased cost of fabric but also because all other costs also had now to be met from a mere hundred styles, instead of the pre-war level of about 3000.

The average Parisian woman wore whatever she could get her hands on, and in winter, because of the shortage of fuel, it was all worn at once. Colourful patches and separate collars were a way of enlivening and repairing old clothes, while trousers at last became acceptable wear for women. Shoe leather was scarce so hefty cork wedges and jointed wooden soles filled the gap. By 1943, it seemed that as the wedge heels became higher, so hats became more exaggerated to balance the look. Based on pre-war designs by Elsa Schiaparelli, hats with small crowns, upturned brims worn forward and to one side were the order of the day. But perhaps it was a deliberate snub to the early 1940s campaign of the unpopular Vichy regime to get all its supporters to wear berets.

Haute Couture Collaborators?

To many in France and abroad, the fact that the fashion houses continued to operate during the war smacked of collaboration with the Nazis. Matters were made worse when pictures of the Paris fashion designs were seen abroad after Liberation: garment after garment in the Paris collections

A street scene in occupied Paris.

seemed to ignore the restrictions and regulations that designers in Britain and the US were bound by. There were cuffed sleeves, pocketflaps, non-functional buttons, pleats and draped fabric galore and dolman (''parachute'' or ''magyar'') sleeves. The foreign press and buyers were shocked and angry.

They weren't the only ones. The American War Production Board immediately proposed press censorship, forbidding any reference to Parisian fashions, ''which are in flagrant violation of our imposed wartime silhouette'', and reminded American manufacturers that L-85 restrictions still applied. No wonder the French government's appeal to the Allied Powers for aid to clothe its population met with a cool response. The Paris designers bowed to the criticisms and the following year limited the fabric in their model dresses $3\frac{1}{4}$ meters (just under 4 yards).

Paris Fights Back

The next task was to reassert the importance of Paris as the centre of

haute couture (high fashion), which began in earnest with the 1945 CSCP's successful traveling exhibition, ''Le Theatre de la Mode'' (the Theater of Fashion), of some 200 dolls (about 2 feet high) dressed by the leading designers that was shown in the West European capitals and New York. The observant fashion watcher that year would have seen the way forward. Cristobal Balenciaga brought his hems down to 15 inches from the floor and by the following year most fashion houses had incorporated the narrow waist of pre-war Mainbocher, a more sloping shoulder line and the accentuating of female curves. But none of this aroused any great excitement or controversy.

That came in February 1947 with the Christian Dior show. He brought all the elements together and gave them a new emphasis. The audience went crazy. Carmel Snow, chief editor of *Harper's Bazaar*, summed it up: ''It's quite a revolution, dear Christian, your dresses have such a new look''. It was these two words ''new look'' that became the way the international press referred to the dramatic new silhouette.

Busy hands – knitting patterns for soldiers.

Top
Cristobol Balenciaga: a dress of 1943. Simple, strong colour combinations, patch pockets, knotted belt, button-through shirt-waist, and yet another eccentric hat.

A wartime day-dress from Jaques Heim. Military looks proved influential in occupied Paris.

Paris chic survived the war intact.
This young cyclist has tucked one
leg of her slacks into her bobby sox,
and wears her hair tied back with a
black band. A blouse completes the
simple but stylish ensemble.

The American Challenge

American Elegance

With the occupation of Paris by the Germans in June 1940, it really did look as if the centre of the fashion world would be transferred to New York. It wasn't just that the pre-war atmosphere in Europe had already caused a few leading designers from Paris to cross the Atlantic to open salons; a number of American fashion houses were already well established and getting coverage in the fashion magazines. Charles James, Norman Norrell and Claire McCardell already had their devout followers, and the return of Mainbocher and others from France seemed to seal it. It wasn't just New York either. Dallas, Texas, was getting a name for sportswear and Los Angeles for casual wear, particularly for the beach.

To many, as well, the fact that the Parisian fashion houses were continuing to operate under Nazi occupation suggested that money spent on French fashion meant dollars in the Berlin treasury. The New York fashion industry did not continue just to follow the lead set by Europe's designers as before. In 1941, six major department stores in New York City showed American designs twice daily, and the race to become top fashion centre was on.

For those ladies wanting elegance and glamour, American designer Norman Norell's sequinned cocktail dresses were the answer, as was the sophistication of Charles James or the drapery of Mainbocher, former fashion editor and editor of French *Vogue*, who had been designing for Wallis Simpson, Duchess of Windsor for many years. These designers had a practical side too. Mainbocher worked on uniforms for women attached to the American Navy and Red Cross and promoted knitwear; while Norell explored the growing ready-to-wear market, concentrating on tailored but waistless jersey shifts (which reduced the use of fabric by 50 per cent) and the separates look of skirt and shirt, which in 1945 developed into the tightly belted waist and full skirt.

Dating at the soda fountain. Casually dressed American boys with a liking for plaid shirts get acquainted with their bobby-soxer girlfriends.

Magnificent McCardell

But the real leader in the American Look, that free and easy style, was Claire McCardell, who like Norell loved the qualities of jersey. She was also a pioneer in the use of unexpected ordinary fabrics, including cotton denim, gingham, calico, and striped mattress ticking. She designed for everywoman and for the everyday world of work and leisure. Her garments were functional and comfortable to wear with dolman (also known as magyar) sleeves, adjustable waistlines, deep pockets, in hard-wearing or easy-care fabrics. Her Popover dress designed in 1943 was basically a wrap-around denim overall, but it looked so stylish it remained a favourite into the fifties. It was classed as a utility garment and within a year 75,000 had been snapped up.

McCardell also hated clumpy, notoriously difficult to wear wedge and platform shoes, preferring to exploit the US rationing exemption on playshoes and ballet slippers, asking Capezio, the leading New York maker of ballet shoes, in 1944 to create an outdoor version of their ballet slippers with stronger soles and heels.

The US government regulations concerning fabric and clothing were quickly lifted after the war. Silk returned for underclothes and evening wear, but synthetic rayon was still used. An important first was the introduction of nylon hose that were totally seamless and very sheer – allowing for a "nude leg" look.

The Changing Silhouette

By 1946 the silhouette began to show definite changes: shoulders may still have been padded, but some were sloping or dropped; and soon natural, unpadded shoulders became very popular. Opinions were now divided on whether women would opt for a new, radically different style of full and longer skirts, or with their new-

found freedom working outside the home, continue to find war-time functional garments more suited to their life-style. In a 1947 article *McCall's* stated: "The short skirt is out of the running. Even before governmental restrictions were taken off skirts, smart girls were letting hems down. The best looking clothes seen walking around New York at the moment are about 15" from the sidewalks. 14" if the wearer is short. No two ways about it, hips are very much in style. The new clothes emphasize round hips by big pockets, gathers and

A two-piece playsuit by American designer Addie Masters in synthetic fabric, 1947.

drapery. Waistlines are small and shoulders are rounded."

However, it was the French designer Christian Dior, supported by the influential fashion journalists, Carmel Snow of *Harper's Bazaar* and Mrs Chase of *Vogue*, who was to settle the argument. With his "New Look" of 1947, Paris was also to regain its position as leader of the fashion world for another decade.

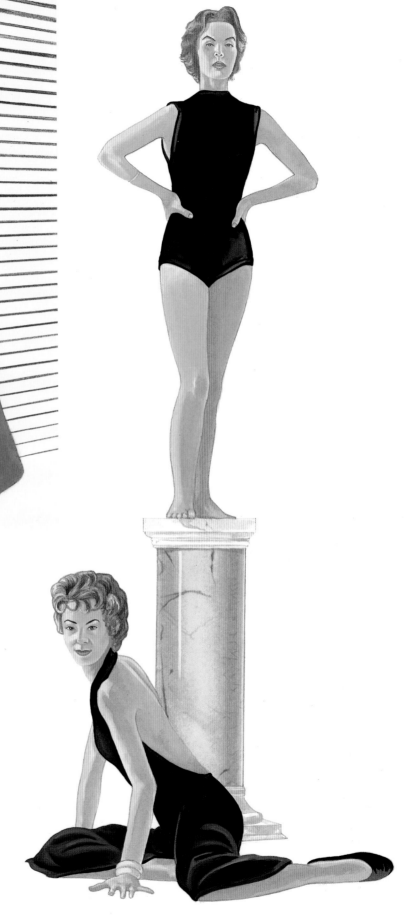

More McCardell inventiveness with stitched denim for casual separates.

Inventive swimsuit and playsuit designs from Claire McCardell.

With money and customers in short supply in war-torn Europe, New York became a haven for the designers of couture evening gowns. These classic and timeless designs are by the Anglo-American Charles James.

British Designers at War

Women in Uniform

The recruitment of women into the British armed services from 1938 meant that new uniforms had to be designed, usually based on those of the men. So, the uniform of the Women's Auxiliary Territorial Service, established in 1938, was similar to that of the British Army and the Women's Royal Naval Services' uniform was modelled on Royal Navy lines, but without the full insignia and markings because, it was argued, the women did not carry out full battle duties. It was recognized that the look of the uniform could affect recruitment and morale. The commander in chief of what was later the Women's Royal Air Force successfully argued against a khaki outfit; blue was thought a preferable colour, partly because of the difficulty in finding cosmetics to match khaki. It was also thought that: ''blue uniforms would not only encourage . . . loyalty and enthusiasm but would also be an aid to good discipline.''

Dramatic changes were seen in the design of nurses' uniforms. The Victorian look, with starched linen – impossible for the battlefront – was increasingly replaced by the simple uniform designed by the British designer Norman Hartnell, while the British Red Cross nurse changed to an easy-to-wash gingham outfit.

Digby Morton, the Irish-born fashion designer resident in London, worked on the outfit for the Women's Voluntary Service. Set up in 1938, the wartime WVS ran soup-kitchens at bomb sites, sold tea at ports and stations for the troops, and organized thrift shops for those who had lost everything in the bombing. Green was originally chosen for the uniform but it was traditionally an unlucky colour, so grey was added to the weave. However, war-time rationing meant few volunteers bothered to wear it.

A Boost for Morale

Morale was also important at home. The British government recognized that stringent rationing could quickly demoralize the population. With only a little prodding, the fashion designers in the country, along with Captain Edward Molyneux from France, were brought together in the Incorporated Society of London Fashion Designers in 1942. Members included Hardy Amies, Norman Hartnell, Digby Morton and Victor Stiebel. Their task was to show that despite rationing, clothes could still be fashionable and attractive. They were to design the Utility collection, stylish garments that conformed to the government regulations. From their designs for four basic items, a coat, suit, afternoon dress and a cotton dress suitable for office work, 32 were selected for production in 1943. The heavy square-shouldered look of the late 1930s was retained, and despite fabric restrictions, jackets and tops had a slightly bloused look. When worn with trousers or skirts lacking any real fullness, and several hat styles based on cap and beret shapes, the designs had almost a military look, although the line was essentially based on pre-war styling.

Can Make It – Can't Have It!

Although deprived of their usual business, that of dressing the British aristocracy – especially in the debutante

Women workers at a spark-plug factory in Britain, 1941. They wear special hats and snoods to prevent hair from becoming tangled in machinery.

season – the members of the ISLFD continued their haute couture work but solely for overseas customers. This had full government approval as the promotion of British designs and fabrics such as Harris tweed brought in badly needed dollars. Peace time brought no immediate change; so the mass of visitors seeing the new ISLFD fashion styles at the Victoria & Albert Museum, in London in the spring of 1946 discovered from the catalogue that virtually everything displayed was for export only. The exhibition's official title ''Britain Can Make It'' was soon popularly known as ''Britain can't have it''.

While American and French high fashion recognized the high quality of British export textiles, the catwalks of the ISLFD salons offered no serious competition to those of Paris and New York at this time. It wasn't just because rationing was still in force. From their memoirs and biographies, it seems most of the British designers preferred to forget this period of austerity; they did not consider it their ''finest hour''.

British *Vogue* gives a war theme to its 1942 high-fashion photo-features.

Utility designs for men and women, 1945.

Wedge heels for wartime wear from the Lotus company, 1941.

Top
Non-utility design. "Just Jane" from the British cartoon provided a comic fantasy relief for troops and others with her scandalous adventures. Here she prepares for the rigours of war in 1940 with a change of clothes – thirties-style evening gown swapped for uniform.

Utility designs by Norman Hartnell, 1945.

Zoot-suiters, Spivs and Zazous

Zoot-suiters

There is still some dispute about exactly where the zoot suit fashion began. The term may have been coined by American bandleader and clothier Harold Fox in 1942. But the style was worn in New York in Harlem by both black and Hispanic teenagers and both groups on the West Coast of the United States also adopted the style. It consisted of a knee-length draped jacket with 6″ shoulder pads, an eye-catching tie (bow or knotted), a long dangling key chain, very high-waisted trousers, fully and deeply pleated at the waist and generous in the leg but sharply tapered at the turnups. The look was completed with a long, greased hairstyle, combed back off the face, a broad brimmed hat and pointed-toe shoes.

Perhaps it was the apparent total disregard of the austerity regulations that the servicemen of Chavez Ravine military base in California took exception to; perhaps there were other factors as well. For two nights in June 1943 they savagely beat up the Mexican zoot-suiters of Los Angeles, cut their hair and stripped off their trousers, while the naval Shore Patrol and army Military Police looked the other way. In his letter to the president, demanding the arrest and punishment of the servicemen involved, Walter White, a political commentator, brought out some of the social aspects of the fashion when he stated that the zoot-suiters dressed as they did "to compensate for the sense of being neglected by society. The wearers are almost invariably the victims of poverty, proscription and segregation."

Zazous

A similar fashion was seen on the streets of occupied Paris among the zazou, street-wise people, who were involved in the black market and general racketeering. It was only through those connections that the men could acquire their huge dropped-shouldered, thigh-length jackets and tight, almost drainpipe trousers, while the women paraded in square-shouldered fur coats, short skirts and striped stockings. Both carried large umbrellas and peered through dark sunglasses whatever the weather. By 1945, a year after the liberation of Paris, the Zazou style was finished and so the second-hand shops in Paris were full of their now unfashionable clothing.

Be-bop casual. Miles Davis knots a knitted tie around an open collar.

Spivs

Confusion surrounds the phenomenon of the British spiv, or wide boy, later immortalized by the comedians Sid Field and Arthur English. It is clear *why* he emerged; he was the small-time black-market racketeer, who for a price could get anything you couldn't find in the shops. So as rationing became more rigorous, he appeared more frequently in the town centres with his battered suitcase or handcart, full with things that had "fallen off the back of a lorry". What is unclear is where the terms *spiv* and *wide boy* come from and whether his

style of dress can be linked with the American zoot suit. *Picture Post* stated that the word *spiv* came from Detroit of the 1920s but others believe it is from the Welsh *spilav* meaning "to push". As for *wide boy*, it seems that refers to the wide chalk-striped suiting material worn by many spivs, first popularized by Edward VIII (Duke of Windsor), but which had fallen out of public favour with his abdication.

The style is usually described as "flashy" but contemporary cartoons show the spiv's suit was well-tailored from good-quality material, whereas the usual man's suit of post-war Britain looked shabby and ill-fitting. The generous wide lapels and double-

Spiv. The youthful Richard Attenborough – later to win Oscars for his film direction – stars in 1947's *Brighton Rock*, as Pinkie, a teenage gangster. Carol Marsh plays Rosie, his manipulated girlfriend.

breasted look of the jacket spoke of money, and was worn with a wide, colourful tie, a little trilby hat (made of felt, with a lengthwise dent in the crown and a narrow brim) worn to one side over the forehead. He sported no flamboyant handlebar moustache, so loved in the war-time Royal Air Force, but instead the tiny, neatly trimmed moustache of Hollywood's Ronald Coleman.

The zoot suit look. Cab Calloway in long, draped jacket, and baggy pants with narrow cuffs and long, dangling key chain.

Trumpeter Dizzy Gillespie sports a Double-breasted suit, goatee beard and black beret.

Be-bop style. Coleman Hawkins and a very youthful Miles Davis. Note in particular Davis's loosely-draped jacket, wide lapels and loosely knotted tie – comfortable as well as fashionable garb for a musician.

The chalkstripe suit for gangsters, or musicians. Wide-brimmed hat and patterned tie provide the essential accessories.

47

Men at War and Peace

G.I. Joe

It wasn't really until American GIs (literally Government Issue but used for American Servicemen) were seen over in Britain that one realized how ill-fitting the British military uniforms were. The GIs all looked like officers in their stylish uniforms. The British field dress with its high-waisted, long jacket and baggy trousers appeared so crumpled alongside. To save cloth and production costs, pocket pleats and pointed sleeve cuffs had been dropped, and the smarter ceremonial dress was out because of the war shortages.

Everyday menswear was also regulated under the British Utility scheme and the American L-85 Order. The only exception was the clothing provided for undercover intelligence officers sent into enemy territory. Such austere styling if worn abroad would have immediately identified the wearers as spies and agents. Some garments that disappeared during the war never came back into fashion. Waistcoats, for instance, took up valuable coupons in Britain and were banned under American restrictions. Short socks introduced to save wool remained in fashion after 1945. The shortage of wool meant very tight-fitting sweaters with a short body length.

Back to Peacetime

With peace, over five million British servicemen were demobilized, that is released from military service. To return to civilian life, each was given a demobilization outfit of a suit, shirt, two collars, two pairs of socks, one pair of shoes, one pair of cufflinks, a

tie and a hat. With the desperate clothing shortage in Britain, the social niceties of wearing a special outfit appropriate to the occasion was largely forgotten. Ordinary, everyday suits, called lounge suits, were now perfectly acceptable for all occasions, and everyone knew that the scarcity of dye-

Generals Eisenhower (USA) and Montgomery (UK) sport versions of the American "reefer" and British "duffle" coats respectively, while observing troops on maneuver prior to the invasion of Europe. Both styles were to prove influential after the war.

stuffs meant lighter tones for suiting material. In the United States, the *New Yorker* magazine illustrated, rather fancifully, seven outfits complete with hats that its returning soldier would need for leisure and work, but which, of course, he couldn't possibly afford.

As rationing ended so men celebrated by selecting double-breasted suit jackets and coats with wide, peaked lapels, so popular before the war. Trousers again became fuller in the leg. Cuffs reappeared, as did unpressed pleats at the waist. At first the trouser waist was high like pre-war styles but gradually it was lowered. Men on both sides of the Atlantic also took to wearing items of military dress: the duffle-coat in Britain and the T-shirt in the States.

A rayon front buttoned dress from Fall 1947, with small box pleats at front and back. Note the influence of men's military uniforms on women's fahion.

1947 sports clothes from California: a checked wool jacket with patch pockets and four-button front, worn with cuffed slacks and a tailored sports shirt.

Duffle Coats

Although Viscount Montgomery of Alamein, British commander-in-chief in the North African, Normandy and Ardennes campaigns, was seen frequently wearing a duffle coat, what made it popular was really the jacket's association with the Atlantic small, fast escort-ships, called corvettes (immortalized in Nicholas Monserrat's novel and the subsequent film, *The Cruel Sea*, 1952). Sub-zero temperatures, and wave-washed decks dictated the duffle's wooden toggles and hemp (rope) loops. Frozen fingers couldn't manage metal fastenings and buttonholes.

After the war, these thick woollen navy coats, named after their original place of manufacture, Duffel in Flanders, were snapped up from military surplus stores. It was only when they began to be worn by university teachers and students, and increasingly associated with the antiestablishment in the late fifties, that the duffle coat lost its heroic aura.

T-shirts

The Japanese attack on Pearl Harbor had the immediate result of putting 11 million Americans into uniform – and into regulation underwear. The following year, the United States Navy sent out its official specifications for an undershirt – calling it a T-type shirt – with a round neck, short sleeves set in at right angles to the front and back panels, made in knitted cotton. At first they were plain white but quickly some were printed with the name of the military base or division.

The pre-war habit of wearing sleeveless undershirts had declined after Clark Gable appeared without one in the film *It Happened One Night* (1934). Suddenly it seemed unmanly to wear that kind of undershirt. The T-shirt saw so much battle-action, no-one could think the same about that. Later a T-shirted Marlon Brando in *A Streetcar Named Desire* (1951) was acclaimed for his "sensual, unfeeling, mean, vindictive performance," and the T-shirt's success was sealed.

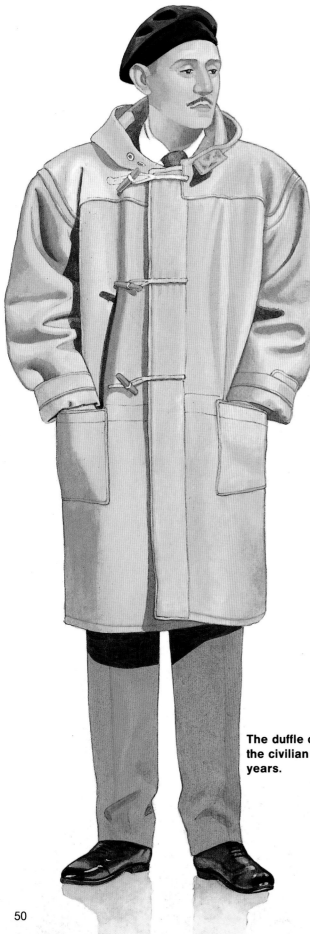

Welcome home . . . for GIs who may have missed the convenience of the soda fountain on service in Europe or the Far East.

The duffle coat – a definite gain to the civilian wardrobe from the war years.

The T-shirt, another military garment that quickly gained a place in the wardrobes of returning GIs.

Hollywood

Impact

The Hollywood studio costume designer had to wrestle with a different set of problems than those of the haute couture houses. Designs had to pass a censorship board called the Hayes Office, set up to guard against provocative costumes, and also conform to the government's austerity programme, as well as conceal or emphasize the physical attributes of the individual star of the silver screen.

Sometimes these devices had resulted in long-lived popular fashions, as for instance, designer Adrian's decision to accentuate the broad shoulders of Joan Crawford in *Letty Lynton* (1932) and *Today We Live* (1933) to make her hips seem narrower. His style of square shoulders and short skirts was so influential that those responsible for drawing up the L-85 Order and Utility program could not envisage women's fashions without padding. It wasn't only the costume designer who created an impact. The filmmaker Howard Hughes is personally credited with having designed the wired brassiere worn by Jane Russell in *The Outlaw* (1943) in order to get the contour and exaggerated uplift he required; he was perhaps too successful as the film was banned for three years because of Russell's sensuous portrayal.

Hollywood Goes to War

War brought its own problems. Hundreds of studio staff were diverted into war work and those who did remain had to work under slashed budgets and other restrictions. The supply of shiny bugle beads, so necessary for the glitzy Hollywood look, was totally cut when Hitler invaded Czechoslovakia where the beads came from. By 1942 studio stocks of fabrics such as brocade,

Deanna Durbin, Franchot Tone, Helen Broderick and Anne Gwynne star in *Nice Girl*? (1941). The big-shouldered look spreads to romantic evening wear.

gold and silver lamé, satin and crêpe were severely depleted and with rationing coming into force, studio wardrobes were ransacked for old costumes that were then taken apart and restyled for new productions. The famous scene in *Gone with the Wind* (1939), still showing to packed cinema houses in the 1940s, in which Scarlett O'Hara (Vivien Leigh) made a dress from green velvet curtains took on new significance. For *Meet Me in St Louis* (1944) there was no alternative but to use rayon rather than silk for most of the costumes.

All Points to Glamour

The most obvious impact of Hollywood was of course in glamour. A picture of Betty Grable in a one-piece swimsuit, looking over her shoulders at the camera, became one of the most popular pin-ups among the American forces; the alluring Rita Hayworth's picture was also a huge favourite. Not every woman had the legs of Betty Grable and not many wanted to have a fruit assortment balanced on her head like the Brazilian bomb-shell, Carmen Miranda, but at least Miranda made the forties turban, so necessary for factory work safety, glamorous. Her wedge shoes too were closely copied by shoe manufacturers. Taste for Latin American frills and off-the-shoulder peasant blouses and "Pacific" sarong prints was further stimulated by the popular Road films (with Dorothy Lamour, Bob Hope and Bing Crosby).

There were less exotic fashions such as Deanna Durbin's white organdy dress in *Nice Girl?* (1941), designed by Vera West, which was copied endlessly for American prom dances; and the rose-covered hats worn in the tear-jerking war film *Mrs Miniver* (1942), which started a fashion that spread eventually to Paris. But other interests, like in lace, following Marlene Dietrich's costume of *Flame of New Orleans* (1941), shrivelled and died with the introduction of the L-85 order. As for menswear, films like

This Gun for Hire (with Alan Ladd) and *Casablanca* (with Humphrey Bogart) ensured the popularity of the trench coat with the belt casually tied and the collar worn up.

Hollywood fashion wasn't always restrained. There were exceptions like the outrageously expensive ranch

Sex symbol. Jane Russell explodes on to the screen in *The Outlaw*.

mink and sequined outfit made for Ginger Rogers in *Lady in the Dark* (1944) and, within months of Germany and Japan surrendering, Hollywood returned to extravagance, as if austerity had never existed.

The designer Adrian was a favourite of Hollywood stars. This outfit typifies the elaborate and three-dimensional tailoring for which he became known. Based on the broad-shouldered silhouette, the suit displays an intriguing, asymmetrical cut.

Armed forces sweetheart. Popular pin-up girl Betty Grable in a famous pose.

Comedienne Lucille Ball poses in typical Hollywood evening wear of the period, with her mane of red hair elaborately pinned up.

That Night in Rio. A Carmen Miranda dance routine and exotic lamé costume.

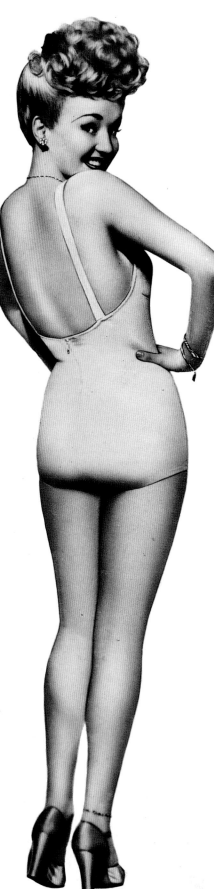

The New Look

Dior's New Look. A tiny waist, tapering shoulders, full three-quarter length skirt and high-heeled court shoes. The overall silhouette could be adapted for day, evening or outerwear.

The Feminine Image

For Christian Dior, his February 1947 collection symbolized a new beginning based on nostalgia for the Belle Époque, a period of comfortable life just before the First World War: "We were emerging from a period of war, of uniforms, of women-soldiers built like boxers. I drew women-flowers, soft shoulders, flowering busts, fine waists like liana [slender vines] and wide skirts like corolla [flowers]." It was a look that symbolized opulence, wealth and a certain image of femininity, in clear contrast to the war-time outline. It was a shape that looked so natural but in reality was totally artificial, with shoulder and hip pads, padded bra and boned waist girdle.

Counting the Cost

It wasn't just the corsetry that caused the temperature of public and government alike to soar abroad; it was the cost and amount of fabric used in making of the skirt, often over 25 yards or 20 meters. Even in Paris women demonstrated, angrily shouting "40,000 francs for a dress and our children have no milk." At the time a school teacher earned 9,000 francs a month and there was still rationing on dairy products, oils and chocolate.

Given that the total amount of material available was limited, estimates showed that the cloth needed for Dior's new length and skirt fullness would bring output down by 800,000 garments (manufactured in regulation style). The President of the British government's Board of Trade warned that the whole future of the British economy was at stake since it would not be possible to make and sell the same number of garments, and he persuaded the British Guild of Creative Designers to boycott the new length. A female member of Parliament, Mabel Ridealgh, denounced the style as "too reminiscent of the 'caged bird' attitude," adding, "I hope our fashion dictators will realise the new *outlook* of women and give the death blow to any attempt at curtailing women's freedom." A female commentator railed in the press "We are back in the days when fashion was the prerogative of the leisured wealthy woman, and not the everyday concern of typist, saleswoman or housewife", pointing out that few British women had the fabric allowance, the money or personal life-style that suited the New Look.

Dirty looks for the New Look in New York! A demonstration is mounted against the extravagant new style for the benefit of Marguerite Cook, model and devotee of the new hemlines, in October 1947.

"Armour-plating." The shoulder pads, wasp-waist corset and hip pads required to underpin the New look silhouette.

Dior Triumphant

But British women in the late forties had had enough of their Utility wardrobes; they wanted change. On hearing the news that rationing was to be continued, Marghanita Laski had summed up their feelings in British *Vogue*: "Patriotism is definitely NOT ENOUGH, and I, for one, am fed up. I'm fed up at home and I'm fed up when I go abroad, I don't like to see a foreigner pointing . . . and whispering 'You can see she's English – look at her clothes!'" And if Princess Margaret, then 17, could appear in public with an extra band of fabric sewn on to her coat hem to achieve the new length, so could others. By 1948 London department stores were selling garments based on Dior's designs for £6 with 15 coupons, and in no time

everything had a New Look label, including daffodils, furniture and housing.

Women in the United States were also hostile at first, though it has been suggested that this was because the new length hid their legs. The American designer Adrian and Mrs Chase from *Vogue* locked horns on American radio over the New Look. Mrs Chase along with Carmel Snow of *Harper's Bazaar* were passionate advocates of Dior while Adrian bitterly criticized the American fashion magazines for suddenly transferring their loyalty back to Paris and welcoming with open arms the reintroduction of heavy corsetry.

He lost the argument, and with it, the United States lost the battle to be the

centre of the fashion world. Paris, led by Dior, had won. Rumor had it that Dior had only included a longer length because it would bring increased sales for his financial backer, Marcel Boussac, the textile industrialist. Whatever the truth was, six years after its establishment, the fashion house of Dior had expanded into six companies, 16 associated enterprises, 28 workrooms and over 1000 employees. The New Look was to influence the world of haute couture for ten years.

Paul Parnes provides an American interpretation of the New Look, Fall 1947. Full length dresses were combined with suit jackets in Parnes's collections for autumn warmth.

Dior's classic New Look daywear. A
tapering jacket with tightly fitted
waist teamed with pleated full skirt,
hat and gloves. About as demure
and ladylike as you can get – and
very far from the fashions of the war
years.

New Look USA. Hattie Carnegie gives her version of the style in 1948. Again the established silhouette, it is the choice of colours and detail decoration that gives this design its individual stamp.

New Look for evening. The same silhouette, with the same attention to detail and accessories.

Glossary

Adrian, (Gilbert) (1903–59) At first known for his theatre and film costumes, dressing such stars as Joan Crawford, Greta Garbo and Katharine Hepburn, he moved into the haute couture world by opening a salon in 1941 in Beverly Hills, Hollywood. He favoured heavily padded shoulders, a clear waistline and clever diagonal closings in his work.

Amies, Hardy (b. 1909) British born, he was known for his tailored suits and lavish ball-gowns, designing for ladies of the British aristocracy and Royal family. While serving in British Army Intelligence during the war, he contributed designs to the ISLFD.

Balenciaga, Cristobal (1895–1972) By the early 1930s he was Spain's leading fashion designer, but moved to Paris in 1936, returning to his homeland during World War II. With his dramatic designs in strong rich colours, he is held by many fashion commentators to be the great innovator of the post-war period.

Balmain, Pierre (1914–82) French born, he worked with Molyneux and Lelong before opening his own salon in 1945. With a reputation for elegant tailoring, he quickly realized the sales potential of boutique accessories and the ready-to-wear market.

Carnegie, Hattie (1898–1956) While employed as a shop-assistant in Macy's, NY, she designed hats, and opened her millinery shop in 1909, followed six years later by a dressmaking salon. Although she herself closely followed Paris fashions, she was responsible for discovering and nurturing the talent of James Galanos, Norman Norell, and Claire McCardell.

Dior, Christian (1905–57) French designer who first worked with Piguet and Lelong. He had instant success with his first one-man collection, the Corolla line (renamed the New Look), in 1947. He continued to exert great influence on the haute couture world until his death in 1957, by which time his salon had expanded into a multi-million dollar fashion business.

Hartnell, (Sir) Norman (1901–79) British designer, showing his first collection in Paris in 1927. Appointed dressmaker to the British Royal Family in 1938, designing both the wedding dress and coronation robes for Princess Elizabeth. He helped found the ISLFD, and a number of his designs were manufactured under the Utility label. Although well-known for his embroidered evening gowns and tailored suits, he also designed the officers' Dress uniform of the Women's Royal Army Corps, and that of the British Red Cross.

ISLFD, or the Incorporated Society of London Fashion Designers, founded in 1942 to promote British fashion abroad and assist the co-ordination between government, manufacturers and fashion houses, particularly during the war years. Besides Captain Molyneux, its chairman for many years, other members included Amies, Hartnell, Digby Morton, Creed and Worth. Very influential in the 1940s, its heyday was in the early Sixties, when British fashion stole the scene.

James, Charles (1906–78) James first entered the fashion world as a milliner, working under the name Boucheron, in Chicago. After moving to New York and then London, he settled in Paris until the outbreak of war in 1939, when he returned to New York. He laid great emphasis on the cut and seaming of garments often working in heavy silks. He retired in 1958 to continue his work as an artist and sculptor.

Lelong, Lucien (1889–1958) One of the first French designers to work in the ready-to-wear sector. He became President of the Chambre Syndicale de la Couture in 1937, a post he was to hold for 10 years, until ill-health forced him to retire and close his salon. It was his skilful negotiations with Berlin High Command which ensured the survival of the Parisian fashion houses. His own salon, which re-opened in 1941, was staffed with Dior and Balmain among others.

Mainbocher (Main Rousseau Bocher) (1891–1976) American designer, who worked in London, Munich and Paris. First a fashion artist and journalist, he then became editor of *Vogue* (French edition) and designed for Wallis Simpson, Duchess of Windsor, before retiring in 1971. His collection in 1939, shortly before his return to the USA, anticipated Dior's post-war New Look. Famous for his ball gowns and evening sweaters, he also designed uniforms for the American Red Cross, WAVES, SPARS and Girl Scouts.

McCardell, Claire (1905–58) American designer, favouring a functional look in practical fabrics, she is considered to have been one of the USA's most influential designers for the Modern Career Woman.

Molyneux, Captain Edward (1891–1974) After gaining experience in a British fashion house, and seeing active service in World War I, he opened his salon in Paris in 1919. His fluid elegant designs were worn by Princess Marina, Gertrude Lawrence and Merle Oberon, among others. Escaping to England at the outbreak of war, he joined the ISLFD, becoming its President, and was a committed advocator of training and education for fashion students. His Paris salon reopened in 1946 but his ill-health forced its closure in 1949.

Norell, Norman (1900–72) American born, he became well-known for his Hollywood and Broadway costume designs from the twenties, and his sequin-sheath evening dresses remained a firm favourite among American society circles for many years. He was the founder and president of the Council of Fashion Designers of America.

Schiaparelli, Elsa (1890–1973) Born in Italy, she lived in the USA until 1918, when she moved to Paris and started designing knitwear. By 1930 she was employing 2,000 people in 26 workrooms. Her approach to fabrics and accessories was unconventional and innovative. A lecture tour of the USA took her away from Paris before its occupation, but she returned in 1945 to re-open her salon, retiring in 1954.

Reading List

Cameron, James *Memory Lane, a photographic album of daily life in Britain, 1930–53*, Dent, 1980

Chase, Edna *Always in Vogue*, Doubleday, 1954

de Pietri, Stephen & Leventon, Mellissa *New Look to Now: French Haute Couture 1947–87*, Fine Art Museum of San Francisco, Rizzoli, 1989

Dorner, Jane, *Fashion in the Forties & Fifties*, Dent, 1975

Flanner, Jane, *Paris Journal 1945–65* vol. 1, London 1966

Minns, Raynes *Bombers & Mash: the domestic Front 1939–45*, Virago, 1980

Mulvagh, Jane *Vogue History of 20th century Fashion*, Viking, 1988

Robinson, Julian *Fashion in the 40s*, Academy, 1976

ed. Sissons, Michael & French, Philip *Age of austerity 1945–1951*, Penguin, 1964

Steele, Valerie *Paris Fashion: a cultural history*, OUP 1988

Lee, Sarah Tomerlin *American Fashion . . .*, Deutsch 1976

Acknowledgments

The Author and Publishers would like to thank the following for permission to reproduce illustrations: B.T. Batsford for pages 8, 9, 16, 17, 19, 20, 25, 32, 37, 40, 45, 49 and 57; The Bettmann Archive for pages 21a and 36; The Hulton Picture Co. for pages 12–13 and 48, The Keystone Collection for page 24; The Kobal Collection for pages 16b and 28; Library of Congress for pages 27 and 63, plus front and back cover; Lighthorne Pictures for page 42; The National Film Archive for pages 52, 53 and 55; Popperfoto for pages 7, 10–11, 12, 29, 31, 33 and 56; David Redfern for pages 21b, 44 and 46; Retrograph for pages 10a, 11, 15, 22–23, 34, 41 and 59; The Vintage Magazine Co. for pages 6, 14, 15, 18, 22a, 23, 26 and 50. The illustrations were researched by David Pratt.

Time Chart

	NEWS	EVENTS	FASHIONS
40	Nazi forces invade Denmark, Holland and Belgium. Paris is occupied British Prime Minister Neville Chamberlain resigns and Winston Churchill takes over	Food rationing begins in Great Britain, and also in occupied France	Schiaparelli takes her collection over to USA; it was to be the last French one to be shown abroad for five years Norell and McCardell steal the (fashion) show in New York
41	Leningrad and the Soviet Union fight off Nazi invasion The Japanese attack on Pearl Harbor destroys 19 ships and 120 aircraft	Aerosols patented First commercial TV networks in USA	The British government bans the sale of silk stockings Clothes rationing is introduced in Great Britain
42	United States enters the war Battle of El-Alamein checks the German and Italian advance in North Africa	Large-scale production of penicillin helps recovery of war casualties	The US government brings in clothing restrictions under the L-85 Order In London, the ISLFD produces the first Utility fashions which go into production in 1943
43	Death camps in Nazi Europe Italy surrenders: downfall of Mussolini	*The Outlaw*, starring Jane Russell, was filmed, but its release was delayed for three years	The British media campaign *Make Do and Mend* starts Claire McCardell's denim "Popover" dress proves very popular
44	Liberation of France by Allied forces	Betty Grable voted top woman film star: Bing Crosby is top male Charlie Parker, Thelonius Monk and others begin classic sound of be-bop jazz recordings	Foreign journalists react badly to the Paris fashion shows. British and American governments ban wide-scale media coverage of the Paris designs
45	US President Roosevelt dies. Hitler commits suicide and Mussolini is shot Nazi Germany surrenders, as does Japan following the bombing of Hiroshima and Nagasaki	American wartime rationing is removed George Orwell's *Animal Farm* is a best-seller	Schiaparelli returns to Paris. Balmain re-opens his salon. Balenciaga drops the hemline to 15 inches off the ground, anticipating Dior's New Look
46	Nuclear tests on Bikini Atoll In Britain, the National Health Service is introduced	The phrase "Iron Curtain" is used by Churchill in a speech in Fulton, USA The word "teenager" is coined in the monthly quality magazine *Mayfair*	The bikini swimsuit is shown in Paris *Britain Can Make It* exhibition is shown in London Molyneux re-opens his salon in Paris
47	Indian independence	Princess Elizabeth marries Philip Mountbatten in a Norman Hartnell dress A Boeing 377 Stratocruiser becomes the first post-war transatlantic plane to carry 50 passengers across the Atlantic	The House of Dior opens with the New Look, which is rapturously received
48	Olympic Games held in London, after a 12-year break The state of Israel is established	First solar-heated house Transistors invented First microwave cookers	Growth of mass-production garment manufacturers, with ranges based on Dior's designs
49	The People's Republic of China is formally proclaimed The North Atlantic Treaty Organization (NATO) is established	First TV westerns A new dance beat – Rhythm and Blues – is emerging	In Britain, clothes rationing largely disappears

Index

Figures in *italics* refer to illustrations.